NOT THE NIGEL FARAGE DIARIES

Published in 2015 by Prion
An imprint of the Carlton Publishing Group
20 Mortimer Street
London W1T 3JW

A CIP catalogue record for this book is available from the
British Library.

ISBN 978-1-85375-924-6

Printed and bound by CPI Group (UK) Ltd, Croydon, CR0 4YY

10 9 8 7 6 5 4 3 2 1

NOT THE NIGEL FARAGE DIARIES

The sort of common-sensical thing Nigel
would write if he wasn't busy planning the
next government!

PRION

Introduction

It was little surprise that the long-standing UKIP leader Nigel Farage was named Man of the Year 2014 by *The Times* newspaper. Despite being limited to weekly appearances on BBC's *Question Time*, thrice-daily interviews on TV news channels and being fêted by just a hundred or so headlines in the *Daily Mail*, *Telegraph* and *The Sun*, Farage broke through the establishment's attempts to ignore him to become a major figure in British politics.

The down-to-earth Farage had got used to being an outsider. He had been raised by a mere stockbroker and his wife in the rough backwaters of commuter-land Kent. It was a tough existence where some hardly knew whence their next round of golf would come. His school – Dulwich College – was looked down on by kids from the more expensive public schools in the country and, like millions of labourers, clerks and plumbers up and down the land, he eschewed university, choosing instead the world of sweat, hard graft and liquid lunches at a commodity broker in the financial heart of London.

A lifelong Conservative activist, Farage left the party in 1992. Despite John Major's introduction of the famously successful Cones Hotline, the signing of the Maastricht Treaty was one step too far for Nigel. Along with his fellow Euro-sceptics, Farage founded UKIP, initially to battle for Britain's independence from European bureaucracy, but increasingly to introduce some common-sense policies to defend the country from an onslaught of politically correct laws; to protect the "British" way of life and ensure there aren't any weird Polish foods in your local supermarket.

As Nigel drives UKIP towards electoral success in 2015, this book provides a fascinating glimpse into the life of a charismatic politician that some have described as the man Enoch Powell could have been if he'd read fewer books on Greek Civilization and spent more time drinking down the golf club.

This book imagines Nigel's inner-most thoughts, envisages what he might be up to as election fever takes hold and makes up some words of wisdom he might possibly write in his diary when he gets back from the boozer...

To-do list...

- Cancel Netflix subscription (nothing worth watching)
- Leave George & Dragon Darts Team (Don't have the time – or the accuracy eh, Bill? Ha! Ha! Ha!)
- Cancel gym membership (Full of gays and scantily dressed women – either one a disaster waiting to happen)
- Leave Old Hedge Fundarians (Not good for me to be associated with them. Pity, though. They're great guys. Reputation ruined by just a few hundred bad apples)
- Cancel *Beano* subscription (spoiled by political correctness – we bullied fat kids at school and it never did us any harm!)
- Leave European Union (Need our national borders back and to gain control over fiscal and other policies)

New Year's Resolutions 2015

1. Lose weight
2. Give up smoking
3. Cut down on the drinking
4. Take a brisk walk each morning
5. Become Prime Minister
   and introduce major
   constitutional reform

Overrun

Visited the delightful village of Within-cum-Cotswold in Oxfordshire. Forced to down a pint of Dogs Bollocks, a local craft beer no doubt brewed by some lefty with a long beard. It tasted like a stagnant pond.

The village is suffering under East European immigration. Yordan, a Bulgarian, moved into a bedsit on the High Street last week but already the village shop is reporting a shortage of pickled gherkins and Izal toilet rolls. "He's flooding this village," a local told me. "The local services just can't cope. I tried to get on the bus to Bicester last week. It was full up but there was Yordan waving at me from the top deck." Another villager reported having to queue behind him at the chemist. "The NHS can't take it," she said. "I was lucky there was any Lemsip left on the shelf after he bought a packet. Extra strength it was too."

Putin

I'm being dogged by the comment I made about admiring Putin. Let's get it straight. I like the determined way the man goes about his business. That's it. I despise his expansionist policies, his oil blackmail of former Soviet satellites and his obsession with being photographed shirtless. Oh, and the clampdown of liberal opponents, how did I forget that one?

Comedian

Pretty annoyed at hearing the news today that some stand-up comedian is going to stand against me at the General Election.

I welcome any addition to the debate, but it is hard to see who is going to vote for this so-called funny man calling himself "Pub Bore" or something. Does he really think that people are going to be taken in by a middle-aged white man, waving a pint around, going on about British values and common sense policies? The electorate are too sophisticated for that I fear.

A woman no less!

Met our delightful UKIP candidate Virginia Borrington-Brite. She seems genuinely loved by the local community, they all commented on how much she has done to improve the local area. A real find. I've been saying how UKIP needs more women to show we have a gentler side.

Liquid lunch of a couple of pints of Spirit of Agincourt at The Old Bull and Bear in the City. Bumped into a pal from my old Hedge Fund company (don't mention the bonus – what the taxman doesn't know!) who tells me they've introduced Casual Friday. He reckons it takes the stress out of the working week by allowing staff to be casually racist, sexist or homophobic without anyone taking offence.

That's just the kind of out-of-the-box thinking that UKIP needs.

The press have revealed that Mrs Borrington-Brite has a criminal record for shooting travellers. Well, not just shooting them. Having them let loose on the estate and hunting them down. I've asked the party to find another candidate.

Brand

Read an article in the *Telegraph* by some longhaired comedian called Russell Brand. I think he's on our side though. He calls me a "puissant sanguinolent with an incommodious dinkel". The lad's either foreign or has swallowed Charles Dickens's set of dictionaries.

Job threat

Nice pint of Scruttock's Blithering Idiot down at the Pig and Calculator in Bury St Edmunds. Very nice crowd, all solidly behind our project. Man behind the bar confided in me that with the arrival of some Eastern Europeans in the area he felt very fearful for his job. I expressed bewilderment at how an unqualified Bulgarian with a loose grasp of English could possibly do a better job than him. Once he'd forgot my order twice, poured a pint with a four-inch head and given me the wrong change, I realized his fears were fully justified.

Sleaze

People have been asking what I am going to do about sleaze and corruption when UKIP finally have some influence in government. As a party recognized as being outside of the Westminster village, I feel it falls to us to help clean up the town. I am intending to put my best man on the case – Sheriff Neil Hamilton. Although now one of us, Neil was in the House as a Conservative and knows just what opportunities are available for a MP on the make or willing to play fast and loose with his expenses. Neil is wise to all the tricks of the trade and naming him as our anti-corruption tsar will show just how serious UKIP are about fighting this poison.

Question Time

Thursday night and I've not been invited on *Question Time*. I ring the BBC and check that there hasn't been a mistake. Apparently they've got Melanie Phillips on and there's a BBC charter quota on the number of right-wing fruitcakes on one programme. I tell them I'm not sure how that affects my place on the panel.

Dumb question time

Was asked today:

"What is your favourite novel, Mr Farage?"

Typical. As the country goes down the drain, the Metropolitan Liberal Elite will talk about anything but the issue at hand. Literature? Who gives one? Of course, my answer of *Biggles Flies Again* didn't go down too well. No doubt I won't be invited back to Highbury Infant School.

Winky

Apparently I was supposed to be insulted by Russell Brand's article. I watched some of his act on television and found very little to laugh at. Since when did talking about your 'winky' replace a good gag about the mother-in-law or the Pakistani family in the local corner shop? Say what you like about Les Dawson but he'd never have left his shirt unbuttoned down to his belly button.

Mosley

Some ghastly socialist in *The Guardian* had been comparing me to Oswald Mosley. What rubbish. I haven't had a moustache since the misunderstanding at that convention outside Munich.

Man of the year

After my triumph in winning *The Times'* Man of the Year award, I was pleased to hear from a trusted aide that I was in the running for Rear of the Year. As a man who takes great pride in his physique, and have received many admiring glances as I walk past, I was honoured to be in the company of Ronan Keating, Olly Murs and others.

Apparently, the aide got it wrong. It was 'Arse of the Year'. I've asked the party to find him another job.

UKIP wit

On a radio debate with the Brand fellow. Thought I got the better of him this time. He called me a "pusillanimous, supercilious knave" and a "Morrison's Own brand Oswald Mosley". I wittily retorted by saying he was 'not very funny' and that 'nobody wanted to see his chest hair.'

Raining again

Didn't the British weather used to be so much better than this? When I was a boy in the 60s and 70s we had traditional seasons. The summer was hot enough to have two weeks uninterrupted tennis at Wimbledon and swim in the North Sea (so I was told – we had a villa in the South of France).

I think it must have something to do with those wind farms. Why on earth would we want to farm wind? Of course, the Common Agricultural Policy is stopping the French from growing sunshine in case it upsets the Spanish.

Euro-lish

UKIP again making them sit up and think in Brussels. We have proposed a policy of a Europe-wide language. We all know that Esperanto was a waste of time so now we are suggesting everyone speaks a form of English. Not exactly as we speak at home but slower, louder and repeated with growing irritation when no-one understands.

Straight talking

BBC *Question Time*. The referendum vote came up again. Lord Someone-or-other started poking the air saying, "There are questions of trade subsidies, transport development, farming quotas, trans-currency regulations and much more. The whole debate on the future of European government is far too complicated to simply fit into an inane sound bite." Smattering of applause from the bussed-in lefties at the back. I replied, "I just don't trust Johnny Foreigner". Standing ovation.

Enoch

Some wet-assed liberal in *The Independent* has been comparing me to Enoch Powell. For goodness sake. Here's a man who the Bishop of Croydon said gave "respectability to white racist views which otherwise decent people were ashamed to acknowledge."

Besides, he was much smaller than me.

Pop genius

Enjoyable day spent with former Radio One DJ Mike Read in his recording studio in Hertfordshire. Mike is at that 'difficult second single' stage and is struggling to come up with anything as pertinent as his brilliant "UKIP Calypso".

A truly talented guy, Mike really is a master of colonial accents. Although just a work in progress, his "All You Need is Love (and a second cousin in Leicester with British Citizenship)" sung in his best

Sub-continental dialect is both hilarious and apt. Just hearing him say 'Poppadum' in that voice makes me crack up giggling – it's probably the best Indian accent I have heard since *It Ain't Half Hot Mum* finished.

Multi-culturalism

Attended a debate on multi-culturalism in Britain. Had to sit through endless guff on so-called contributions to science, art, and the richness of society. Finally I was able to put forward my argument that multi-culturalism has been a total failure. "How often," I asked. "Have England reached the quarter finals of a major football tournament since Labour's open door policy?" The Metropolitan Liberal Elite have no answers to hard facts like that!

Job description

More irritating questions from smug BBC reporters about employing my wife as my secretary. I told them there is no point my advertising the post as there is no other woman who could do the job. It is precisely that she is my wife that she makes such a good secretary.

My previous secretaries have baulked or quit when asked to undertake perfectly necessary secretarial tasks such as typing a last minute report, making me a cheese sandwich late at night, cutting my toenails, speaking in that sexy German accent and smelling my farts under the sheets.

Weighty matter

UKIP debating our policy of a return to pounds and ounces. A lot of common sense being spoken. "No one in this country has grasped grams and kilograms," said our proposer. "You just don't know what to ask for down the market'. He went on, "Before all that European nonsense, everyone knew there were 16 ounces to a stone and 19 pounds to a ton. It was so much easier to work out.

Breast or...

I received a disturbing report from one of our members who had a shocking experience at a London restaurant. While waiting for his steak to arrive, my colleague noticed a woman on a nearby table adjusting her dress around the cleavage area. Now, I know him well and he's well accustomed to taking a sneak peek whenever he gets the chance, but he was aghast when she produced a sprog and started giving suckle at the table.

Worse was to come. When he called the manager over to point out the indiscretion and see the woman escorted off the premises, he was shocked by the reaction. "Sir," said the restaurateur. "If you are the sort to take offence at such natural behaviour I would ask you to put your napkin over your head or retreat for a while to the restroom. Please consider our other customers," he added. "No one wants to look at a tit while they are eating." That's London for you.

E.U.F.U.!

One of our moles in Brussels yesterday revealed that the EU President has formed a committee just to come up with policies to annoy Britons. My source tells me they've already suggested...

- Changing the name of the English Channel to the Franco-German Canal
- Taxing profits from Tombolas at country fairs
- Outlawing queuing in shops and public institutions
- 'Sunday Roast' signs in pubs to read: "Weekend Oven-Cooked Animal Produce with Fat-drenched Potatoes and Boiled Vegetables"
- Closing DIY stores on bank holidays

Mugabe

In trouble with the press for saying I admire Robert
Mugabe. Contrary to what they are saying it is not his
anti-gay policies I endorse or his methods of chasing
unwanted ethnic groups out of the country. I was
simply referring to his golf swing, which I glimpsed on
a BBC documentary. I believe he plays off 17.

Terrorists you can trust

I was just trying to make a point about foreigners
in this country. Most are innocent hard-working
people just going about their business trying to milk
our benefits system for anything they can. Hardly
any of them are terrorists. Unfortunately, they all
look a little like they might be. Who can blame
people for assuming that anyone who speaks a bit
funny or looks like they work in a halal butchers is
planning to blow them to bits?

Say what you will about the Irish terrorists we had in the 70s, but they integrated well into society. You could be sitting in a pub having a drink next to an Irishman and you wouldn't even think about calling the police until they opened their mouth.

Mussolini

What will they come up with next? Some idiot in a homeless persons newspaper has been comparing me to Italian Dictator Benito Mussolini. For heaven's sake! The man used his party's minority position in a coalition government to create havoc and secure ultimate power. Besides, he was a much heavier set man than me.

Candidate

Met our prospective candidate for Bickerstaff East.
Ageing but charming old chap with an accent I
couldn't quite place. He had all sorts of fascinating
and progressive ideas covering the local rail networks,
youth organisations and immigration.

Fox News no-go

Interviewed on *Fox News* this afternoon. They were
interested in my views on no-go areas in Britain.
They were shocked to hear that there were parts of
London, Bristol and even Leeds where ordinary,
decent people are reluctant to go. They feel like
foreigners in their own country. The menus in cafes
are incomprehensible and the shops are full of
unrecognisable foods such as rocket, tofu and kale…

There are no pubs, just bars serving quirky-named craft ales at extortionate prices and with a DJ in the corner wearing a hoody and their pants showing. Fried chicken outlets are scarce, having been replaced by Vietnamese wrap stalls and burrito bars and there are no bookie shops, just mysterious cultural buildings called 'libraries'.

The streets are patrolled by a 'Police' force of men in check shirts on fixed wheel bicycles intimidating those without full beards. Outsiders are sneered at for their brick Android phones, they feel obliged to keep their copies of *The Sun* hidden and at any moment expect to be pulled over for driving a petrol-driven van.

Soundbite follow-up

I've been trying to replicate the success of my greatest
soundbite: "The UKIP fox is in the Westminster
hen house". I dismissed Carswell's suggestion of
"The UKIP hand is up Westminster's skirt" and
whoever suggested, "The UKIP plonker firmly up the
Westminster bunghole" needs shooting.

Nein, nein, nein

Turns out our Bickerstaff East candidate was the son
of notorious Nazi Klaus Spurtel AKA the
Haberdasher of Hoffenheim. I've told the local party
to select someone else.

Taxes

Lunch with an old chum from the investment bank. They've been having a bit of trouble from the Pay Your Taxes protesters. I told him I paid enough tax on my gin to keep them in benefits for years! Apparently the great unwashed want to put a stop to overseas investments. Sounded pretty reasonable to me, but they don't mean Europe – they're talking about my cash in Bahamas and the Cayman Islands!

I thought they only had banks over there so there was a handy branch in case I went on holiday. Then he explained. Honestly, what kind of free society is it where an honest broker can't squirrel his client's hard-earned millions away from the taxman in a virtual account in the Caribbean?

Big hoo-ha in the press about UKIP's Empire Officer calling his Chinese chum, Fu Manchu (Well, I think he was Chinese, could have been Japanese? Which way do the eyes slant again?)

Had my wife (or secretary, if the EU or HMRC are listening!) call Gunga Din, Hu Flung Dung and Paddy Mulligan (real name but you can't be too careful) and tell them to deny ever meeting me.

No fair

The fairground has come to Tunbridge Wells, so I took the nephew down to get him sick on candyfloss and centrifugal force. I could not believe the queues. An hour for the rollercoaster, 40 minutes for the giant tea cups and even a 10-minute wait to catch a plastic duck that wins two points towards the 50 needed for a cuddly toy.

Oh for the days before Albanian benefit tourists filled up the waltzer cars and breast-feeding Bulgarians took all the places on the Big Dipper. Is it just me who yearns for the days you could be innocently pick-pocketed picked by a young Gypsy boy or randomly abused by a Brylcreamed Irishman?

Transfer window

Heard a bit of Westminster gossip today. Apparently The Tories are really running scared at the sheer number of their members transferring to UKIP. Word has it that they are thinking of introducing a football-style transfer window, which will close three months before the election.

Plumbing

Interesting meeting with the newly-formed Great British Plumbers Association. Our homegrown plumbers are rightly concerned about the flood of migrant workers from Eastern Europe. Unqualified, and with little knowledge of the vagaries of British plumbing, they are undercutting native tradesmen, doing an efficient job and clearing up afterwards.

"This is not what our customers are looking for," said Dennis, the Association's President. "What they have come to expect is for our members to turn up late, tut and scratch their heads for a good half an hour and rummage around in their tool bag until they are offered a cup of tea. This is how customers know they are getting a professional job. He added, "Some of these foreign guys don't even spin the job out for five minutes to notch up another hour's call out time."

Hoxha

In trouble with the press for saying I admire Enver Hoxha, dictator of Albania from 1944–1985. My quote was taken out of context. For the record, I do not condone his Stalinist methods of destroying associates who threatened his own power and neither do I admire his policy of economic isolation. I merely admired the crazy paving he had installed in his driveway in a photo I saw of his mansion outside Tirana.

Hard-working

On walkabout in Gloucester. Was taken to task today by my promise to ensure that the hardworking British people are the priority for any government UKIP are involved with after the election.

"Fair enough," the gentleman said. "But all the parties say that. I want to know who's going to look after all the lazy f***wits like me?"

Gives the party a bad name

Was shocked today by the revelation that UKIP
has more men called Dave or Steve than women
standing for the party in the election. This really is an
unacceptable situation and I'm urging the party to do
all they can to get them to change their names.

I wonder where we get some of
our members! Some idiot in
Basingstoke has just been quoted
as saying "How can they say we're
a party of racists? We've got
just as many misogynists and
homophobes too."

Trap!

Another day, another speeding ticket. Not sure how many more points the wife can put on her licence (just a little joke for my old friend Chris Huhne, Officer!) It's an appalling trap. They hide the bloody things in just the places where you want to put your foot down. What's the point of having an expensive Jag if you have to pootle along behind some social workers in a Punto? It's political correctness gone mad. After all, what kind of country are we living in where you get punished just for breaking the law?

Pot noodle

Wish I hadn't made the remark about reminiscing
fondly about Pol Pot. In response to those who have
made certain assumptions, I would certainly not
consider replicating his extermination of intellectuals
or his forced evacuations of ~~the Metropolitan Liberal
Elite~~ city dwellers to harsh rural labour. It had been
a long day, I had had a couple and I was actually
thinking of Bill (or was it Ben) the Flowerpot Man.

Bog standard

Forced to use a public toilet as I did a walkabout in Chelmsford (at my age once you've 'broken the seal' after a few pints at lunchtime, you're pointing Percy at the porcelain every half hour or so). Made me wonder quite what has happened to the great British bog? There was a time when every public convenience had a room where a little retarded chap with a cap sat and did *The Sun* crossword. He'd be suitably submissive and keep the place clean. Nowadays you have to shuffle past a huge trolley pushed by a big-skirted African woman only to find a stinking refuge for drug takers, gays, cyclists and other unsavoury elements. It's like a breath of fresh air when someone actually comes in for a pee and even the graffiti isn't written in English anymore.

Up North for a meeting with our prospective candidate for Cleckthorpe and Braithwaite constituency.

Thank God we have plain speakers like Ralph Halfbottom in the party. Ralph's a good solid Yorkshireman – no airs and graces – says he calls a spade a spade (we both smiled a bit uneasily at that bit) and doesn't mind who knows it. I for one can't wait to see him putting the wind up those "softy Southerners" down in Westminster with his tell-it-how-it-is honest bluster.

Fruitcake

Our UKIP election strategist has been on the phone. He's concerned about the proliferation of small right-wing parties that are springing up across the country. He's especially worried that we could lose out as, in his words, "they split the fruitcake vote". Wasn't exactly sure what he meant, but apparently there's a significant number of unhinged racists, bigots, neo-Nazis and xenophobes out there who could be willing to desert us and vote for them. It appears that some of these parties pretend to have a raft of moderate policies but are actually just a front for some nasty anti-foreigner ideology! Politics, eh?

Ralph's mouth

Had a call to make to my new friend Ralph Halfbottom. The *Yorkshire Evening Times* headline story featured some choice words from Ralph about Green Party members' sexual relations with the local sheep. I'd assumed he'd been misquoted but Ralph assured me "It's t' bloody truth. Everyone round here ha' seen it for thee selves." I asked him if he was sure it was a Green Party member and he said, "Of course I'm sure, lad. He had a bloody Parka on." I've asked the party to replace him.

Talking shop

Marvellous photoshoot over a pint of Enoch's Revenge with our candidate in Accrington South. He tells me that none of the shopkeepers within a mile radius of his house are able to conduct a conversation in English! He was obviously reticent about making such a remark but with some glee I reveal this fact to the sceptical local press (a bunch of lefty journalist work experience types).

Shopped!

Interesting follow-up to our candidates claim that none of our Accrington candidate's local shopkeepers can speak English. One of the local journalists investigated and discovered that they can all speak perfect English (one is a retired professor from Cambridge) but because our chap is such a boorish oaf, they just pretended in order to avoid having a conversation with him. Got the party to tell him to mind what he says in future.

Wales

Been out on the streets of ~~Clnn, Cllr, Crn~~ some unpronounceable town in Wales, where our UKIP vote is holding up very well. It's hardly surprising. The people there have suffered terribly from the influx of Eastern Europeans. Their English way of life has been diluted and distorted. You just have to look at all the signs in town. Not only are they written in English, they are also spelled out in some unpronounceable foreign language. I even wrote down one message scribbled on a wall, "Cachau bant Farage!" it said. I can't find it in my Polish-English dictionary.

Single issue

I've become a little worried that there is only one aspect of our manifesto that our supporters are actually interested in. UKIP have policies on many issues confronting modern Britain, but could it be a single factor is causing them to vote for us? As much as I agree with our policy on lowering the price of alcohol, we have many proposals on issues such as immigration, they might want to consider.

Fellow UKIP members,

When dealing with the media please refrain from:

- Discussing UKIP policies. When we have some we will let you know.
- Discussing your political background. It's probably a bit iffy so best keep quiet.
- Discussing immigration. You'll only use words you'll regret later.
- Discussing homosexuality. Don't. Just don't say anything. Please.
- Try to mumble as inaudibly and meaninglessly as possible between the following words... **Immigration** blah, blah, blah... **NHS**... blah, blah, blah... **Local Services** blah, blah, blah... **Brussels**... blah, blah, blah **LibLabCon** blah, blah, blah...
- Finally, please don't go on national TV spouting nonsense on behalf of UKIP. That is my job.

Was on some London commercial radio station discussing terrorism. It's very hard trying to make a serious point about fifth column fanatics in our midst when you are interrupted every 20 seconds by an advert for an exhaust fitters in Harlesden or a "Have You Had an Accident at Work", solicitor.

New Friends

Off to Brussels. I actually rather like Belgium. Loved those Tintin books as a boy. Can't quite remember the titles... *Tintin in the Evil Socialist Empire*? Tintin *Fights the Fuzzie-wuzzies*? All cracking books anyway. Just a pity they put the EU there.

Off to meet with the new alliance we've set up for groups around Europe who, just like UKIP, are challenging the established parties. Some of them are quite small but feel we have lots of common aims such as eliminating bureaucracy, cutting the size of the state and giving the poor old smoker a break. I didn't catch all their names but I did write them down...

All good moderate Euro-sceptic parties I'm told.

Netherlands - Immegrent
                Oost Naaw
France - Le Front Raciste
Germany - Die Führer Risen
Sweden - Weit Freedholm
Italy - Fascisti Glori

I can't speak their lingo but they all seemed like
smashing chaps.

Unsocial media

Had to send a memo around about the use of social media. Many of our members think their messages are private and are unaware that they can be read by anyone. It's so easy to be misunderstood and for an off-hand comment to be taken out of context. The wrong thing gets out and it's Muggins here, who is red-faced, stuttering and blinking furiously in front of Nick Robinson.

Julia Likely, our Port Vale West candidate...

Quite innocently posted "Had coffee with my Czech*
neighbour, Marta. A delightful lady who when not
working nights as a locum surgeon, takes a shift in
the local Help the Aged." Well-meaning, I'm sure, but
it's not going to win us any more votes from ~~frothing-
at-the-mouth~~ concerned citizens.

Also, took part in debate on the demise of
Britain. How, I asked, has such a proud nation
which once boasted the best armed forces, public
schools, seaside resorts, and motorway service
stations in the world, sank so low? Even our football
hooligans struggle to take on the Police force of a
small Eastern European country's these days.

* NB: she informs me that Czechoslovakia no longer
  exists. When the hell did that happen?

55

Inter-national health service

UKIP committee meeting on the National Health Service, or as one of our members hilariously called it "The International Health Service". He told us of the appalling number of immigrants he came across in his local hospital. A Ugandan gave him his bath, a Sri Lanka administered the anaesthetic and even the bloke on triage had a strange accent. Another added that there is a problem with the language spoken in the NHS. Three times he had corrected his doctor's pronunciation of "burst appendix". It was only on the way for emergency surgery, that the medic seem to realize where the inflection was supposed to be.

Can-do Dave

Splendid afternoon in the local Evesham hostelry with UKIP candidate for Evesham East Dave (didn't catch his last name).

Dave's the kind of can-do guy that typifies the UKIP spirit. No Health and Safety worrying, Equal Ops fearing, do-gooding, political correctness for Dave. He just gets right out there and does what's best for party and country. What a guy! Did an interview after five or six pints of Worcestershire's own Charlatan's Folly and told the local news crew how they could trust Dave and that he was definitely – *definitely* – my best mate ever.

Costa del UKIP

Spent tonight in the studio of *The Essex Show* on Romford Radio. They had a live link-up with Radio Benidorm. Glad to hear that UKIP has plenty of support from the ex-pat Brits out on the Costas. George from Marbella rang in from his sun bed to complain about those foreigners coming to Britain but unwilling to work; Marjory and the other English pensioners in the Generalissimo Franco Ward at Marbella General wanted to say how mass immigration put such appalling extra pressure on services in the UK and all the lads down the Red Lion pub and Terry's Fish and Chips shop in Malaga agreed it was the way those from overseas refused to integrate with British culture that presented the major problem.

Told the party to make sure those postal votes get sent out pronto.

Can-do/don't do

The local news has revealed that Dave, our Evesham East candidate, has been getting his leaflets delivered by some local Bulgarians. Had to point out to him that there is a difference between "can-do" and "taking the piss".

The local news has revealed that UKIP's Evesham East Bulgarian leaflet distributors are Dave's cousins. Dave said he wanted to be an MP and UKIP seemed the best bet. I should have taken notice when he said his surname was Borisov. Told local news he is no longer my best friend and had a word with the local party organizer about finding a new candidate.

Off the rails

I hate having to go on the trains in London. Having travelled down to Kent from the city last year I remarked on feeling awkward at hearing no English spoken in the carriage. Not going through that traumatic experience again, I thought, as I stepped onto the platform for the 19.25 to Tunbridge Wells.

This time I plumped for the silent carriage. It was just as bad. All around me people were texting in foreign, looking at strange languages on their laptops or playing strange versions of Angry Birds on their iPads. And those without technology were frowning in a foreign way, staring out the window in an oppressive East European manner or smiling to themselves at some obscure Slavic joke. What a relief when someone with a suit got on at Pett's Wood and listened to Adele loudly on their phone.

I get such little time to myself
these days but managed to get
in the Jag and run down to the
coast for a pint of Ebb Tide.
Just the one of course, the
Establishment all think we turn
into crazed speed monsters after
a pint and a half.

Annoyed to find the road was half
closed and there's a half-a-mile
tailback. The problem? They're
putting up a 'Toads Crossing'
sign. This government! They care
more about rare toads than your
ordinary motorist on the road.
And why do these toads choose
to cross on a busy A road? No
wonder they are rare.

Gaddafi

Mark Reckless has been bigging up former Libyan dictator Colonel Gaddafi for stopping boats travelling across the Mediterranean Sea to Italy. I understand what he means but had to tick him off. We can't go around admiring vicious dictators – even if they weren't all bad.

Amin

My comments have been taken out of context again! When I said we could learn from Idi Amin, I was not referring to his ethnic persecution, corruption or nepotism in secretarial appointments. I merely said I had a good omelette recipe my uncle had picked up from the former President of Uganda.

Eurovision

Watched our sorry effort flounder at the *Eurovision Song Contest*. It is surely not helped by many of the other countries singing in their own language. Have they changed the rules? No wonder the Eastern Europeans are doing so much better now we don't get to laugh at their poor accents and odd vocabulary.

Enjoyed a couple of pints of
Kilroy's Revenge with our
Berwick North candidate. Lucky
sod. He only had a grandfather
who died in the war. So useful
when it comes to gaining the
moral high ground.

All in this together

Someone has written an article about me, focussing on the Cult of Personality. They claim that I am the only one driving UKIP forward and without me the movement would wither. What nonsense. The party is full of dynamic and inspirational characters. For example, there's Nuttall, (admittedly a bit of a loose cannon), the baldy Tory defectors and, well, I can't remember the others' names. But the point is I am just the spearhead of the party. An instrument to achieve what we strive for. The party's tool to get us out of Europe. Nuttall only said to me the other day, "Farage," he said, "You are a complete tool."

Had a tricky meeting at HQ today. It turns out that the average age of our party members makes the local bingo hall look like a nightclub. No wonder we're dropping off in the polls - by the time the election comes around half of them will be dead.

Berlusconi

Whoops! OK, I did admit I held a smidgen of jealousy for former Italian Prime Minister Silvio Berlusconi. Of course, contrary to received wisdom, I wasn't referring to his ability to get away with financial indiscretion or his convenient alliances with dodgy right-wing groups. I just thought he must have some good chat-up lines.

Ideas to attract young people to UKIP

- New youth-targeted slogans: UKIP – it's wicked!, UKIP U-Cool!

- When on TV use language the young people will understand...

  - "We've got like a banging new policy that like deals with da pikeys and that."

  - "That Mark Reckless is some sic dude man, innit!"

- Promote UKIP-supporting celebrities that the under 25s can identify with. For example, Radio 1 DJ Mike Read, glamour pin-up Joan Collins, TV scientist Patrick Moore (if he is still alive).

- Young people use social media to communicate. Friends Reunited, the Facepage thing, email... er, does anyone know any others?

- Sponsor a stage at a festival, like Glastonbury? Get some trendy bands to play under our logo. Thinking of combos like The Hermans Hermits, Peters & Lee or Anita Harris?

It's all academic

Who do I hate nearly as much as the Metropolitan
Liberal Elite? Eastern Europeans? I hear you guess.
Nope. Muslims. 'Fraid Not. Eurocrats? Well, almost.
Travellers? French? Pregnant Women? Phone Shop
Assistants? Cycle couriers? Tee-totallers? ... OK, that's
enough guessing. Who said academics?

In their ivory tower universities, these so-called
intellectuals have no idea of real life. They sit there
collecting statistics such as "people from counties
in eastern Europe contributed £5bn more to the UK
economy than they received in benefits." Typical.
Facts like that don't advance the argument. Ordinary
people's real life observations are what count. Hardly
a day goes by when I don't hear something like, "I saw
a bloke signing on today – he looked a bit Bulgarian.
Well he had a funny moustache anyway." or "they've
started selling a strange brand of baked beans in my
local corner shop". Stick that in your thesis, Prof!

Why Sevenoaks should be the new capital of Britain

- Nearer the South Coast – we can keep an eye on the French
- Only foreigners are the ones working in Pizza Parade
- Only a 20-minute train journey from major hubs, such as Croydon and Tunbridge Wells
- It is further away from Scotland
- Has a number of fine Shepherd Neame pubs
- Europeans don't know where it is
- Nobody there buys *The Guardian*
- A proliferation of golf clubs in the vicinity
- Will boost area of real hardship – some houses have only increased 250% in value over the last two years.

Target Seats

1) CRABGATE AND PARKINGTON-ON-SEA

Constituency: East Kent coast. Prime UKIP country. Mobility scooter tailbacks on the high street and pound shop proliferation. 75% over 60-year olds, some South East London white flight; smattering of 80s 'alternative' benefit seasiders and a handful of depressed middle-class families who gambled on gentrification and are now just grateful for the grammar schools.

Local issues: Immigration, funeral prices, lottery numbers.

Candidate: Dave Clewless. Former Conservative backbencher nobody had heard of, who suddenly became front-page news when he came over to us.

Random quote: "Who's a jumped-up covert-racist twerp now, Cameron?"

They say: Conniving careerist turncoat with a grudge.

We Say: Sidelined maverick genius given his due.

Opposition: Labour has blown it since their Highgate

MP tweeted a picture of someone's shopping basket with white bread, Doritos and ketchup. Tories are resorting to going round old folks' homes telling doddery seniors that they're voting for Margaret Thatcher. There is a Lib Dem, but he's hiding.

2) CHILDENHALL

Constituency: Suffolk. Rural area full of red-faced farmers and company directors who drive to London twice a week in the Range Rover. Considerable concern about influx of Bulgarians. They prefer Albanians. "They be much cheaper," said one local farmer. So conservative they don't even bother to vote. 3% turn out at last election.

Local issues: Immigration, hunting, manure prices.

Candidate: Dave Bergamot-Prance. Former president of Young Farmers' Association (East Anglian Branch), Master of the Suffolk Hunt, founder of Blood Sport For All. Once arrested for chasing down anti-hunt protesters with dogs and horses – and explosives.

Random quote: "The EU thing yes, but what about the hunting repeal?"

They say: Blood-lust farmer fighting for a single issue.

We say: Local guy sticking up for local concerns

Opposition: Softly softly catchy monkey. Should be a walk in the park as long as no one wakes the Conservative blue rinsers up. Labour has packed up years ago. The Greens have a stall on market day. School kids giving away apples. That'll win 'em votes!

3) ROMLOW

Constituency: Essex New Town. Once Labour stronghold. They lost it in the 80s, won it back with Blair, lost it again and have now forgotten where they put it. Angry hard-working people always treated worse than everybody else. Angry about tax, housing, transport, NHS, fuel prices, TV reception, England's world cup performance, behaviour of children on buses and decreasing size of Wagon Wheels.

Local issues: Immigration, cars, everyone else getting stuff.

Candidate: Dave Tunt. No career politician here. Dave is new to politics. He stresses he is not the Dave Tant who was former leader of the local BMP or Dave Tung, former leader of the local National Front branch. Dave says his interests are collecting wild flowers and contemporary dance.

Random quote: "If you say that picture of that guy in the KKK outfit is me , I'll ***ing do you."

They say: Illiterate former skinhead with anger management issues.

We say: Rough diamond with a heart of gold and interesting policy ideas.

Opposition: Labour is gaining in polls with voters angry at NHS cuts. The Conservatives are still strong from people angry with Labour. Lid Dems voters are angry that no-one is getting angry or is the slightest bit bothered about them.

4) SKIDLINGTON

Constituency: Humberside. Former fishing port once home to proud fish processers at a well-known fishfinger company. Now most work for Japanese assembly plant, having to attend morning meditation and eat raw fish for lunch.

Local issues: Immigration, fishing quotas, people south of Sheffield.

Candidate: Dave Toggle. Former Conservative mayor, turned Labour MP, turned Green MEP, turned Monster Raving Loony Police Commissioner Candidate.

Random quote: "I am honoured to be standing on behalf of the Labour, no, Tory, no wait, er..."

They say: An opportunist candidate who will stand for whichever party might get him elected.

We say: An honest local candidate who has become frustrated and disillusioned with traditional parties.

5) IBROX NORTH-EAST

Constituency: Glasgow suburb. Strong SNP support. Upset about not leaving Britain but we can offer next best thing – leaving Europe. Need to support candidate by sending up some kilted UKippers who can put on a good Scottish accent.

Local issues: Immigration, independence, Irn Bru.

Candidate: Dave McSmith. Despite being brought up in Hertfordshire, McSmith considers himself fully Scottish. He has a Scottish great-grandmother and a penchant for shortbread. Previously stood as a 'Keep Scotland English' candidate (lost deposit).

Random quote: "Och aye folk. I have a dream. I have a dream that one day my children will be able to watch Glasgow Rangers playing Arsenal, Manchester United and Hull City in the English Premier League."

They say: "The UKIP candidate has no interest in Scotland. He is not even Scottish – he's just added a 'Mc' to his name to make it look like it."

We say: "Scotland needs to reject control by a foreign capital and exit the EU."

Opposition: Like a bride jilted at the altar, the SNP are garnering the sympathy vote. We need to remind voters that the enemy are Eastern Europeans and Muslims who steal our jobs, not the English – there should be no place for bitter, small-minded nationalism in these isles. Surprisingly, Labour is in with a shout – these people have short memories on account of the drink. The Tories are like the Loch Ness Monster – some claim to have seen one, others say it's just a myth to scare the children.

6) ISLINGTON WEST

Constituency: The beating heart of the Metropolitan Liberal Elite. The only people who can afford to live here are BBC Producers, *Guardian* journalists and owners of organic vegetable box delivery services. Social housing is filled with middle-class single parents roughing it and refugee hordes from God Knows Where. Our hope is the decent British through-and-through Afro-Caribbean community.
Candidate: Delroy (aka 'Dave') Douglas. A former

Olympic weightlifter, dandy and all-round eccentric. Delroy was UKIP's first black member (Note to Party HQ – do we have any more yet?). A well-known local ~~laughing stock~~ figure, Delroy cuts a dash in his velvet suit, cane and top hat. Seen by the party as a valuable, if unpredictable, asset.

Random quote: "I can't be UKIP 'cause I'm black? I tell you sir, I'm as racist, homophobic and bigoted as any of their bloody white men."

They say: He is just a token black candidate who UKIP are exploiting for publicity.

We say: Delroy proves how welcoming our party is to all fair-minded Englishmen (and those born in the former colonies with reasonable claims to stay here).

Opposition: The Lib Dems were a big noise at the last election but now they all avoid them like the clothes aisle at Tescos. Greens are in fashion along with Hunter wellies and iPhone 6s. Most of the population have been to at least one dinner party, played tennis or given the kids a lift to drama school with someone from the Labour front bench.

7) WEST WORKSOP

Constituency: Middle England. One of the few places in the country where people's votes actually count. These voters are very anti-Europe, anti-Westminster, anti-London, anti-East Worksop... They don't even like their next-door neighbours very much.

Local issues: Immigration, house prices, whatever is on front page of that day's *Daily Mail*.

Candidate: Susan Bitecock MEP – "the Battle-Axe of Brussels." Famous for her campaigns: "The EU want to stop you eating chips", "The EU want to take your pets away" and "The EU are coming for your first born".

Random quote: "The EU want to ban hopscotch because it's not fair on one-legged children."

They say: Scaremonger; forever making up lies to smear the European Union.

We Say: Pitbull MEP, keeping a watchful eye on EU directives.

Opposition: Current MP is a one-nation Conservative. Well-liked by a constituency who wouldn't know him if he punched them on the face in the high street. Labour candidate is some parachuted in barrister from North London who is willing to make the tiresome trip from Islington twice a week to further his career. Interesting independent fighting on a "Leave Europe but join the Pacific Island Forum for closer links with Tonga and Fiji" ticket.

Half-baked

I need to get a grip on party policy. Sometimes it seems like I pop into the pub and by the time I come out someone's decided on some half-baked policy I have to turn up on *Newsnight* and get all hot under the collar about. Arrived at party HQ today just in time to prevent them putting out a press release on plans to provide shoeshine boys at every major station.

Farage's Foreign Affairs

I've been fortunate in my work as a MEP to have visited many countries in the world. They're not all bad! Around the world I've encountered marvellous scenery, fantastic cities, fabulous food and interesting people – all courtesy of some pretty generous, but thoroughly legitimate, expenses.

Contrary what the sneering liberal elite might say, I don't dislike foreigners. Not if they stay in their own country, don't try to undercut British workers and make some kind of attempt to speak English when addressed. Indeed we have much to learn from them. I often say we could do with a little of the French insouciance, the German's self confidence, the American love of their flag, Swiss driving laws, Australian bloody mindedness, Belgian chips and the Serbian's willingness to confront ethnic difference.

I've written to ITV suggesting I present a travel guide for like-minded people on holiday on the continent – something like *Farage's Foreign Affairs*.

A kind of *Lonely Planet/Rough Guide* for people on expenses who don't want to live off rice and sleep in municipal campsites and makeshift brothels. On this basis, I've made a few notes to show the TV execs...

France

A once beautiful country now reduced to a holding pen for immigrants waiting for the chance to jump on the back of some unsuspecting British day-tripper's booze-filled Fiat Uno.

Still under the impression that Napoleon is in charge, they think they are Europe's grand fromage. Fortunately, they are more of a Babybel. The French carry no weight in the EU, are of even less importance in NATO and don't even count for much in France these days.

There has been much discussion lately of 'no go' areas in Paris. I have witnessed these personally. You don't have to travel far beyond the tourist sites in the centre to feel isolated and threatened. On a recent visit to the edge of the 9th arrondissement, I stumbled across a Muslim enclave. The people there were clearly not French but nevertheless still couldn't speak English. Moreover, it was nigh on impossible to buy a copy of the *Telegraph*.

In my time in the corridors of power in Brussels, I have come across a great deal of French people. On the whole I fund them small-minded, parochial, xenophobic with a tendency to react hysterically to small problems. If they weren't such cheese-eating surrender monkeys, they might be perfect UKIP members.

Switzerland

"How will we ever survive without the economic opportunities of the EU?" bleat the Europhiles. I suggest they peek over the borders of their beloved France and Germany to Switzerland. Mrs F and I love a romantic trip to Switzerland – all that mountain air and chocolate can make up for a lot of late nights ironing my shirts and filling in expenses forms.

Although basically a big lake and lots of mountains, Switzerland somehow gets by very well on exporting cheese, chocolate and multi-tool penknives. You just have to look at BMWs rolling down their motorways to see they are not exactly suffering the effects of austerity.

They are helped, of course, by their marvellous banking system. There is much to be said for an ask no questions, hear no lies financial policy. So their vaults are full of Nazi gold? What if a few African dictators syphon off their country's GDP into a personal account? So they harbour a few chancers who plot devastating attacks on nation's economies for personal gain. It's no business of ours and as an old banking chum of mine said on his terrace overlooking Lake Geneva, "Listen Farage, either we have a nice country you can come and visit or join the EU and they'll give our cash to a load of sweaty Greeks? What would you rather we did?"

Spain

Anti-UKIP moaners often use the number of British ex-pats living in Spain as an argument for EU migrants living in Britain. There is of course a difference. Britons in Spain offer invaluable skills in timeshare villa sales and their culture is all the richer for bars showing English Sky Sports and serving strong lager on draught.

Of course, there is more to Spain than the coast. I discovered Granada, a lovely city dominated by the Alhambra Palace. This is a charming and beautiful building spoiled only by the Arabic daubing, probably wishing destruction of the country that welcomed them – have they no respect for tradition?

Like us the country is suffering from youth unemployment, immigration and the excesses of too much liberal rule for too long. You can't help feeling what they need is the firm and authoritative rule of a military general.

If the naysayers want to see what Britain might look

like under UKIP they need look not much further than Gibraltar. It is a country with low crime levels, British bobbies on the beat, red telephone boxes and offshore tax-haven banks – Paradise.

Like other European countries Gibraltar suffers from the multicultural issue. They endure a community who will not integrate, eat vastly different foods and whose cultural habits are disgusting to those raised in the British way. As brutal as it seems, culling them is possibly the only way forward. Alternative steps are underway to deport the troublesome Barbary monkey community back to North Africa are being undermined by EU bureaucrats.

Germany

I like Germans (I have to say that or there is hell to pay when I get home). Us British and the Germans have much in common. They are rational, reasonable, hard-working and like a good sausage. The difference between us, is that they are German and will therefore try to take over the running of Europe every now and then. We will nobly resist, and in our struggle save the continent for which we will receive scant thanks – again.

Germany's cities – Hamburg, Berlin and Munich – are refreshingly modern. They seem not to have been blighted by the English disease of 'listing' every building over 80 years old regardless of how ugly they are. It is as if they have knocked the whole place down around 60 years ago and built the whole thing up again. Marvellous planning.

At the fall of the Berlin Wall, thousands flooded over from the East. The West has coped admirably; assimilating these people into their country. Imagine dealing with an influx of poor people from a different nation who look and talk the same! You wouldn't even be able to point them out on the high street, complain about them on the bus or ask them to work for next to nothing.

I Wouldn't Want to Live Next Door to...

A group of Romanian builders

Unemployed foreigners

Married gays

BBC Producers

A wind turbine

I Like Living Next Door to...

White van drivers

Stockbrokers

Bankers

Billionaires

Dear Mr Juncker,

As I am shortly to become an MP in the House of Commons, I am writing to inform you of my resignation as a Member of the European Parliament.

I would like to say it has been fun, but I must be honest. It has been as much fun as having my teeth pulled. I've chewed through countless pencils while sitting through endless meetings about milk production in the Austrian lowlands. I've got neck ache from nodding at the incomprehensible English of some delegate from some god-forsaken Silesian mining town. And, my nostrils are still keeling from the truly astonishing smells emanating from some representatives of the fruitier nations in the general council.

Moreover, it has been costly. All member states are paying a premium for the inadequacies of the Commission. This is a disgrace. There is no control or accountability over the EU's spending. While on this matter I would like to refer you to a number of my MEP expense claims that are still outstanding.

Dry Cleaning after Green party 'compost' protest €675

Hotel Bill (mini bar and Channel XXXX) €3,438

Dry Cleaning after Estonian sewage protest €146

Office Stationery (pens, pencils, little fluffy creatures that go on the end of pencils) €3.75

Dry cleaning after French pig farmer's 'manure' protest £347

Grecian 2000 €456

Mrs Farage (secretarial and other wifely duties) €743,000

Dry Cleaning after Belgian Dry Cleaners' Union protest €453

Pizza delivery €798

Ear buds €98

Big jobs

It's wrong to say that we won't accept overseas citizens into Britain. If their skills are such that they can fill vacancies here, of course they will be welcomed onto these shores. Here's my list of jobs foreigners should be allowed to do...

- Be my secretary/wife – No British person will ~~put up with me~~ have the skillset and organisation skills that come naturally to the Germans.

- Be the Queen's consort – The Greeks have a track record in this sort of thing.

- Play in goal for Chelsea – The astute, handsome, billionaire Abramovich is just the kind of donor supporter we need at UKIP.

- Play for England's rugby or cricket team. It is important for national morale that we do well in international sporting competition. In the absence of decent home-grown players, UKIP would extend the tradition of allowing anyone who has a grandparent who lived in Britain to play for the national team to those whose relatives, however distant, once came on a holiday here.

- Set up ethnic restaurants in provincial town high streets. The sub-standard Indian, kebab and Chinese takeaway is now as much a fabric of our local towns as churches, schools and charity shops.

- Pole dancing. Until we train up sufficiently skilled young women of our own to humiliate themselves in front of lecherous, drunken businessmen, we will be forced to rely on imported labour from Eastern Europe. I particularly like Czech girls – just saying.

- Acting. Playing foreigners in TV dramas and comedies is a tricky business. Unfortunately though, every actor seems to be able to cry and shout, few share the range and ability of, say, Mike Read in mimicking accents.

- Mini cab drivers. Our British young drunks want nothing more than a stooge at which to target a torrent of vomit and racist abuse in the early hours. Our own black taxi drivers are in bed at this time – they have an early golf round booked.

Saving our pubs

Our pubs are dying out. Two out of ten won't still be open by Christmas and the ones that are will be more interested in serving slow-roasted boar with a raspberry coulis than a pint of bitter.

It's no wonder really. Alcohol tax and Health and Safety have knocked the character out of these places. Me and a team at UKIP have been knocking our heads together for ways to save the traditional British Boozer:

- Pipes and a pouch of heavy shag to be provided to all men over 50.
- Pubs to display peanut dispensers that reveal more of a picture of a scantily clad woman as more packets are purchased.
- Smoking to be reintroduced. And made compulsory.
- Introduce common-sense drink driving laws. Drivers stopped should be able to tell police "know when they've had enough".

- Breathalysers will not include half pints, whisky chasers, a swift "couple" after work or Sunday lunchtime drinking.
- State-subsidized Friday lunchtime strippers. Finished in time so women can pick their kids up from local school.

Why the Great Multi-cultural experiment has failed

- You can't find the Branston pickle for all the chutneys on the shelf.
- The woman in the local shop didn't laugh at my 'Four Candles' joke.
- The man in the post office couldn't spell 'Nigel'.
- The flush is broken in the toilet in Carriage F on the 8.12 from Sevenoaks.
- You never see white dog poo on the pavement any more.
- I still have to go all the way to Maidstone for a decent curry.

Punk rock party

At UKIP we pride ourselves on being the outsiders – a threat to the establishment. We're the Punk Rock Party – we say what we want and don't care what anyone thinks. Yeah, I like a drink, a smoke and hanging out with the boys from the banks. I admit I'm a little bit of a rebel; I sometimes wear my yellow socks with brown trousers. It's rather fun and I'm in good company.

Just thought I'd jot down a few of my anti-establishment heroes who inspire my work…

- Paul Nuttall – my right hand man. Great thinker. Just wait until the Metropolitan Liberal Elite hears his ideas about ~~privatizing~~ modernizing the NHS.

- Michael Heseltine – Tarzan knew how to put it up 'em. Back when the Tories had some spunk, the young Farage idolised the flaxen-locked wild man of politics.

- Les Dawson – he took on those alternative comedians and won! I could spend hours watching re-runs of his hilarious mother-in-law jokes and out-of-tune piano playing.

- Dave Hedgington-Snedgington – I used to work alongside 'Hedge Fund Hedgington'. "Rules are for losers" he'd say. Made millions. Out of solitary now and I still see him occasionally when I can swing by the prison.

- Jesus – The well-known biblical figure not the Manchester City winger.

UKIP residency test

A focus group have been looking at the UK
Residency test. Not sure the current questions
are sifting out the right calibre of skills, IQ and
cash reserves ethnicity. We need people who truly
understand what it means to be British, understand
our history and culture and get enough questions
wrong to be refused.

They've put forward some jolly relevant questions:

a) Who was the left back in England's 1966 World
   Cup winning team?

b) What do you need if you feel a little p-p-p-p-
   peckish?

c) Page 3 model Vanessa from Bristol's interests
   include watching Chelsea, ornithology and doing
   what with her twin sister, Vicky?

d) In less than ten words, write a mathematically
   complete example of a quantum gauge theory in
   four-dimensional space-time.

Twitter guidelines

- Always state your credentials: "I've lived here 30 years", "I'm not racialist but..." "I've got old fashioned values so... "My Grandad fought a war so..."
- Your beliefs are "common sense" and "decent"; ones you disagree with are "Politically-correct nonsense" or "Westminster spoutings".
- Try to mention Asylum Seekers, Benefit Tourists, East Europeans and the Metropolitan Liberal Elite as much as possible.

Useful hashtags:

#OverstretchedLocalServices

#ControlledImmigration, #GlobalWarmingCult

Banned Hashtags:

#IlefttheBNPforUKIP, #GaysMakeItRain

Remember: There is no longer a Rhodesia, Third Reich or National Front.

Remember the big picture: For instance, when commenting on a football match try something like: "Great performance by Arsenal's Wojcek Szecney. Pity his compatriots don't earn their money too."

Ideas for responses to difficult questions about our policies...

- I don't know where you got that idea.
- It was just an idea we discussed at the party conference, we discuss many things.
- That was a policy, but the party has moved on
- That wasn't a policy, it was just one of "Nutter" Nutall's "ideas".
- That wasn't a policy, it was just something I read in a Christmas Cracker.
- We scrapped the 2010 manifesto in its entirely.
- That isn't a policy, we just like winding Ed Balls up.
- We scrapped the manifesto we wrote after we scrapped the 2010 manifesto.
- We don't really have policies – they're such a Westminster 'thing'.
- ~~We only really have one policy – the immigrant stuff – the rest is what you might call garnish.~~ DO NOT USE THIS LAST ONE!

UKIP - party of culture

Who said we are a party of philistines? Our members just loved the million or so ceramic poppies displayed at the Tower of London for the First World War anniversary. Patriotic, British and proud. How unlike the obscene, self-indulgent and incomprehensible nonsense that passes for art these days. Ukippers up and down the country have been discussing what other public art would enhance rather than degrade this great country. They've come up with some jolly interesting ideas...

- An Angel of the Midlands – Big woman holding a Melton Mowbray Pork Pie.
- A 'No Entry' sign painted on the White Cliffs of Dover.
- Statue of Andy McNab.
- The bricking up of the Channel Tunnel.
- Symbolic 'Rivers of Blood' installation in Birmingham.

NHS

When Ed Milliband said there is only one issue the British people are focussing on at this election, I thought "Hello!" Ed's got it at last. Then he said it was the "H" word.

I love these games so I started thinking. Er... Hungarian? Himmigration? Nope. I gave up. Turned out he meant "Health". Next thing I know they're all going on about the NHS. So, I thought UKIP better have a policy...

- The NHS is safe with us.
- We have no intention of privatizing the Health Service.
- Rumours that Nutter Nuttall has already put the NHS on eBay, starting at 99p, are unfounded.
- The branded 'Virgin' ambulance was not our idea. Honest.
- No more postcode lottery. Waiting lists will be drawn up according to:

a) How much you donated to UKIP

b) How many indignant letters you have written to the *Daily Mail*.

c) How far back you can trace an immigrant-free family tree.

- Our immigration policy will not affect the service. The 88% loss in surgeons will be covered by staff from Dewhirst, the Butchers.

My top British beers...

* Scruttock's Old Bunglings
* Dribblesome Scrapings
* Galahad's Droopp
* Valiant Defender (19°)
* Swilly's Swiller
* Sir Crispin's Dragonblood

My top foreign beers...

*Rheinheitscroat is it? - I can't even spell it!

*That monk-brew dark beer they sell in Belgium. No wonder they don't wear pants - that stuff goes right throught you.

* Um...

NHS

Red Ed Milliband has been spouting on about his "Mansion Tax" again. Mansion! He means hard-working ordinary people's homes. There are some round my way who would suffer and all they have is a six-bedroom mock Georgian house and they still have to keep the golf clubs in the second garage.

If he wants class war – we're ready to go after him and his chattering class . I've asked the party for suggestions for what we should tax and as usual they are full of cracking ideas.

UKIP Tax ideas

- Fixed-wheel bicycles
- Olive oil
- Beards
- Recessed lights
- eBooks
- Three-wheeled buggies
- Rocket
- Organic vegetables
- Free Trade Coffee
- Independent cinemas
- Prius Cars

QUESTIONNAIRE

Do you think the party you voted for last time are a complete shambles?

Do you think immigration is the most important issue?

Are you concerned about Britain's laws being made in Brussels as well as not liking immigration?

Do you think education and the health system are priorities – but just not quite as high priority as immigration?

Would you like to vote for a nutcase right wing party but feel you are a bit 'better' than that?

Do you get upset if someone calls you a 'racist'

Do you think things aren't as good as when you were young?

Does it upset you to hear people talking foreign on the bus?

Do you still feel a bit suspicious about the Germans?

Do you get political correctness and health and safety confused?

The French – they're not like us, are they?

Are you sick of the same old Westminster LibLabCons?

Nevertheless you would be happy to vote for people who used to be in one of those parties and only very recently left?

If you get red in the face and shout "Yes, I bloody do!" at these questions, then UKIP is the party for you.

Nexit

The whole idea of leaving the EU has been a great
vote-winner for UKIP. I really don't know where the
party would be if we hadn't came up with it. So I've
been setting my mind to what else we might leave.
None of them seem to have that 'EU' factor but worth
thinking about…

Things UKIP could campaign
for Britain to leave:

- The European Ryder Cup Team
- The International Cricket Board
- The British Isles and Ireland
- The Geneva Convention (If no-one
  else is going play by the rules…)
- The Eurovision Song Contest
- BBC4 (European subtitle channel)

School days

The press have been digging around my old school, talking to boys I don't have the foggiest memory of and teachers who were a bit doddery even then. Nevertheless, I find it a little hard to stomach coming from the old college.

"I recall Farage spent most of his time trying to persuade his class to leave the rest of the school."

"Farage was vociferous in blaming the class's poor performance on Josep, the new Polish boy."

"When he was a prefect I had to stop Farage locking a first year in the cellar for a week. He complained it was political correctness gone mad."

"Farage was elected to the school council but seldom turned up. He was, however, the only councillor to try to claim expenses."

"I sat next to Farage in Geoggers. Nightmare. He'd cut out Britain from the wall map and pasted it way up in the North Sea near Iceland."

"In music we had to sing Simon and Garfunkel's 'Bridge over Trouble Water'. Farage walked out saying it was 'a load of lefty nonsense'.

"I remember a history class when Farage said, 'Churchill was right. We should have fought Russia when our troops reached Berlin.' He then argued, 'and then we should have annexed Poland and come back and taken on the French for good measure.'"

Future goals

It is the duty of the leader to look to the long as well as the short term of the party. Ever since our formation, UKIP has worked towards one main goal – Britain's exit from the European Community. So as that objective nears its successful completion, where should the party turn it's attentions now?

The party sent out a survey to this effect and obtained some interesting results. To the question: Which issue do you consider the party should focus on next? They received the following answers…

Lower Taxation 29%
Housing for Local People 24%
Corporal Punishment for Schools 12%
Capital Punishment for Schools 11%
Bring Back Blue Police Boxes 8%
Bring Back Black and White TV 7%
Re-join Europe 7%
Embark on Apocalyptic anti-Islamic Crusade 2%

See your face

When I heard about our bold move to ban non-stun slaughter of animals, it seemed brilliant. It was a fabulous way to give our halal-eating Muslim friends a nudge towards civilized British slaughter methods. And, this time, nobody could accuse us of being racist – we're just supporting the RSPCA! Then I get a call saying the whole Jewish community (many of them good UKIP people) were up in arms. Apparently kosher meats are slaughtered in the same way. Who knew?

This new idea should fare better:
No veils or face coverings to be worn in a public place. I've checked with a local rabbi and we're on safe ground here. One of the baldies is set to announce the policy tomorrow.

Scrapped that policy. Deluged with complaints from brides, beekeepers, motorcycle couriers and Batman costume providers. Too much of a vote loser.

The earth moved

Last week's earthquake in Kent was pretty shocking.
Measuring a massive 3.2 on the Richter Scale, it
shook tea cups, led to it getting a bit choppy down
Folkestone way and made me miss a putt on the 8th
at Hythe (which was really a gimme, but "Ron 'Atko'
Atkinson don't play like that!").

Now I'm sure if this wasn't England, but the Indian
sub-continent, there would charity appeals, fire
brigade units flying out there and the government
doshing out aid left, right and centre. But we're
British. We pick ourselves up and get on with it. We
don't cry for help for broken crockery or refunds for
bets with racist-comment tainted former football
managers.

A little more research did however get me
thinking. Apparently, Britain is prone to these
disastrous, or at least inconvenient, earth tremors,
because it is part of the Eurasian Tectonic Plate.

Typical of LibLabCon that they saddle our isles with a volatile sub-surface favored by not only the French and Germans but the Indians and Pakistanis too!

The way forward is clear. On achieving its aim for Britain to leave the EU, UKIP will campaign for us to leave the corrupt and unreliable Eurasian Tectonic Plate and go it alone. Free to join the American Plate or link up with the Australian Plate, Britain will once again prosper without the fear of hearing faint rumbles, noticing hairline cracks in the living room ceiling or having some overweight, cigar-chomping former pundit chortle at you.

Wind bags

Had a letter from our Cumbrian members. Sick of
the proliferation of wind farms despoiling the natural
beauty of their area, they have produced a map of all
local wind farms and details of how quickly they can
be disassembled. It's a fine local effort that as part of
their campaigning tools, will reap dividends in the
election.

Changing climate change climate

UKIP remain the only party for the climate change sceptical voter. We insist the jury is still out on the global warming issue. Nearly 3% of scientists agree with us and if that isn't enough to take the Volvo out for a spin I don't know what is. UKIP has a unique and refreshing place in its attitude to science. Here's a few other things we are sceptical about.

• The moon is over 250,000 miles away. Really? I can see it most nights and I can't even see Tunbridge Wells and that's only three and a half miles away.

• Wind farms provide over 10% of our fuel! Green Party garbage! I drive by regularly and those propellers are hardly ever turning round.

• Dinosaurs? Great big bodies – tiny little arms? I don't think so.

• Recycling. It's a big myth. I've been putting my stuff out for years, but still haven't seen anything made of a baked beans tin, a shoebox and a wine bottle.

Frack off!

I have received many replies from the 'Fracking' questionnaire sent out to UKIP members. Almost unanimously they back the party policy endorsing fracking, wherever we might scent a trace of the black stuff. They did express certain reservations about where we might concentrate the fracking work.

A prospective MP from Liverpool and Manchester for example, wrote, "Essential we begin fracking as soon as possible. Unfortunately, the North West is over-populated and ill-suited to such explorations." Our West Riding candidate was equally enthusiastic. "Let's get drilling as soon as possible – but avoid vulnerable areas of natural beauty such as the North York Moors."

Our Essex members are forthright: "Ignore the protesters and Not-In-My-Backyarders, fracking is in the national interest. Do it round here though and the bloody Tories will win every seat."

Finally, a frank missive from our Cheshire MEP. "The damage caused is completely exaggerated. We cannot be hypocritical. Start in Cheshire. I have no fears for fracking in my constituency. I visit twice a week from my home in Llandudno and I'm sure the locals won't mind.

Electric shock

With some gusto I was telling a local meeting about
the Cumbrian wind farm map (see page 116) and
their plans to destroy the useless ugly things. It was
met with some silence. "Hello!" I thought. Has there
been a change of wind direction over the whole wind
farm issue? It turns out I hadn't seen the local news.
The Cumbrian map featured electricity pylons instead
of farms. For God's sake! No one minds thousands of
huge metal monstrosities littering the countryside –
it's the small propeller ones we don't like. Idiots.

UKIP Transport Policy

- We will scrap HS2 but introduce HS3 (London to Sevenoaks), HS4 (London to Colchester) and HS4a (London to High Wycombe).

- We will require foreign visitors to drive electric smart cars. Not for any environmental reason but just so we can laugh at them.

- Bus fares will be kept low, but passengers will be required to wear a badge saying, "I can't afford a car".

- Speed cameras will be remodelled to give you a wink if you are just exceeding the speed limit and to flash "Wow! Great driving!" if you reach a ton.

- Tolls will only be charged to keep the traffic moving. They will be paid by cyclists, old men with hats, tractors and cars towing caravans.

Overseas Aid

The reckless spending of UK taxpayer's money in overseas aid is something UKIP have long campaigned against. Every time someone around the world stubs their toe our government can't wait to pay out. We give aid to India, even though their cabinet still has biscuits with afternoon tea, and food aid is sent to Indonesia despite the proliferation of reasonably priced restaurants.

UKIP will send overseas aid only when and where it is urgently needed. Here are the places we feel need it most at the present time.

1. The Algarve, Portugal. Many of the golf courses are struggling to maintain their greens to the standard required for a decent round. Water is often a scant commodity and is unfortunately diverted to local homes instead of where it is most urgently required.

2. The Costa Del Sol, Spain. British ex-pats are struggling to cope with the escalating inflation in Spain. It is hard to stand by when they do not have the money to get their swimming pools cleaned on a regular basis.

3. Canvey Island. This once glamourous-ish seaside resort is now a shadow of its former glory. Our overseas aid can pay for a spruce-up and a decent marketing campaign.

4. The Isle of Wight. Can we really stand by while fellow citizen's caravans need modernizing and Wi-Fi connection? Some of them still do not have electric hook-up. Shocking.

5. The Falkland Islands. They don't need any money, but it's fun to piss the Argies off. The look on their faces every time we build a new barracks or government building is worth every penny!

Dear Dave,

Many thanks for your letter. I perfectly
understand your deep upset and shock and
I hope you are feeling better now. I'm
sure many of us would feel similarly if
confronted with the sight of two middle-
aged men shopping together at our local
supermarket.

UKIP are naturally against "that sort
of thing". We would do not wish to make
homosexuality illegal, but would hope
that those practizing the depravity would
feel like it is. Some great men from our
history: Cecil Rhodes, Alan Turing, Alec
Guinness managed to be homosexual without
skipping down the high street holding
hands.

I must however take issue with some points
in your letter...

• I would be grateful if in future you
  stick to the term "gay" when describing
  these people. Some of your terminology,
  while extremely graphic and amusing,
  was probably a bit much.

- Until it is scientifically proven, we cannot claim gays cause floods and other natural disasters; delays on the East Coast line; poor performances by the England rugby team; unexplained coned-off lanes on the M62 or the extortionate prices of seats at West End musicals (although you may have something with this last one).

- To my knowledge, doctors are not able prescribe pills to "straighten them out".

If you do not heed these guidelines, I will be forced to reconsider your post as UKIP LGBT Officer.

Nigel

P.S. I assure you gay women do actually exist. They are not, as you write, just made up for mucky books.

New Oath of Allegiance

I .... (*insert your name here – if it doesn't fit – neither do you*) thank every British person for the gracious invitation to become a second-class citizen in this green and peasant land.

- I swear allegiance to the Queen (she's the woman whose face is on the coins).

- I honestly really, really love the Queen and all her hangers on, even the truly annoying ones called the Duke of Whatever who don't do anything useful.

- I promise to obey all her Majesty's government's laws. Furthermore, I will not question the House of Lords as an unelected assembly but instead gush about a great institution and ask "But what could possibly replace it?"

- I will henceforth refer to the armed services as 'Our Lads' and only speak of them in hushed terms of awe and pride.

- I will support Britain's sporting teams no matter how dire they are. I will not laugh when they fail to qualify for international tournaments.
- I will not talk loudly in a foreign language on the bus.
- I will not cover my face with a veil and will smile when requested to do so by groups of men in passing vans.
- I will queue for goods and services but give up my place to someone who looks proper British.
- I promise not to use the NHS unless I have something contagious real British people can catch.
- I will not undercut hard-working tradesmen who own their own van and, anyway, are only charging a little extra to pay for a three week holiday in Florida.
- In the event of snow, I will moan endlessly about how unprepared the authorities are.

Nigel Farage

UKIP Headquarters

10 Downing Street

London, SW1A

UK, The British Isles, The World.

Dear Mr Juncker,

It is with great delight that I
write to inform you that Britain is
preparing to free itself from your
confederation of idiots and thieves.
We wish you the best, as a prosperous
Europe will benefit us all (good luck
in getting your money back from the
Greeks and the Spanish!)

Regards,

Nigel